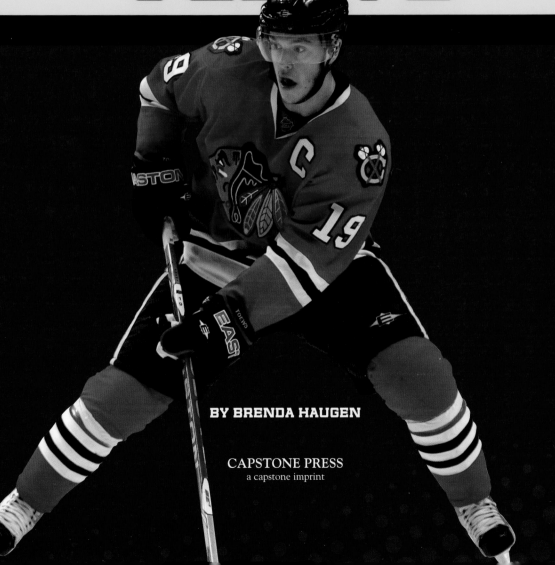

D1308853

★ HOCKEY SUPERSTARS ★

# JONATHAN TOEWS

### BY BRENDA HAUGEN

**CAPSTONE PRESS**
a capstone imprint

Sports Illustrated Kids Hockey Superstars are published by Capstone Press, 1710 Roe Crest Drive, North Mankato, Minnesota 56003. www.capstonepub.com

**Library of Congress Cataloging-in-Publication Data**
Haugen, Brenda.
Johnathan Toews / by Brenda Haugen.
pages cm. — (Sports Illustrated Kids. Hockey Superstars.)
Includes bibliographical references and index.
Summary: "Details the life and career of hockey superstar Jonathan Toews"—
Provided by publisher.
Audience: Age: 9-10.
Audience: Grade: 4 to 6.
ISBN 978-1-62065-157-5 (library binding)
ISBN 978-1-4914-9024-2 (paperback)
ISBN 978-1-4914-7605-5 (eBook PDF)
1. Toews, Jonathan, 1988—Juvenile literature. 2. Hockey players—Canada—
Biography—Juvenile literature. 3. Hockey players—United States—Biography—
Juvenile literature. I. Title.
GV848.5.T64H38 2016
796.962092—dc23
[B]                                                                    2015010713

To my hockey family, Mike Meyer, Mark Brown, and Dan Brown. I love you all! BLH

**Editorial Credits**
Jack Manning, editor; Terri Poburka, designer; Eric Gohl, media researcher;
Tori Abraham, production specialist

**Photo Credits**
Alamy: All Canada Photos, 9; Courtesy of Shattuck-St. Mary's: 11; Getty Images: Jonathan Daniel, 1, 7, Scott A. Schneider, 12; Newscom: Icon SMI/Robin Alam, 25, MCT/Charles Cherney, 14, UPI/Brian Kersey, 5; Sports Illustrated: Damian Strohmeyer, 20, David E. Klutho, cover, back cover, 16, 18, 23, 26, 30–31 (background), 32 (background), Robert Beck, 28
Design Elements: Shutterstock

**Source Notes**
Page 6, line 15: Associated Press. *Blackhawks 7, Canucks 5*. Canucks.com. 6 Aug. 2014. 15 March 2015. Canucks.nhl.com/gamecenter/en/recap?id=2008030246
Page 8, line 8: Dan Rosen. *Toews and Canadian Tire make a perfect marriage*. NHL. com. 20 Aug. 2010. 15 March 2015. nhl.com/ice/news.htm?id=536214

Printed in the United States of America in North Mankato, Minnesota.
032015      008823CGF15

# TABLE OF CONTENTS

CHAPTER 1

# AN EPIC BATTLE

The Chicago Blackhawks and Vancouver Canucks were locked in battle. They were playing Game 6 in the 2009 Western Conference semifinals. Chicago was up three games to two in the best-of-seven series. One more win and the Blackhawks would be headed to the Western Conference finals. They also would be one step closer to winning the **Stanley Cup**.

Vancouver opened up the scoring about 11 minutes into the first period. But thanks in part to a goal and an assist from **center** Jonathan Toews, the Blackhawks climbed to a 3-1 lead midway through the second period.

Vancouver was down but not out. The Canucks knotted the game at 3 before the end of the second period and grabbed the lead in the third. Chicago rallied to tie the game at 4-4 only to see Vancouver score again less than seven minutes later. Then Chicago's Patrick Kane answered with his second goal of the game to tie the score at 5-5 just 45 seconds later.

With less than six minutes left in the final period, Vancouver was called for a **penalty**. Chicago was going on the **power play**.

**Stanley Cup**—the trophy given each year to the NHL champion

**center**—the player who participates in a face-off at the beginning of play

**penalty**—a punishment for breaking the rules

**power play**—when a team has a one- or two-player advantage because the other team has one or more players in the penalty box

Chicago fans were in a frenzy during the third period. At times the crowd in Chicago's United Center was so loud the players couldn't hear their coaches. Soon fans had even more reason to cheer.

Less than 30 seconds after the power play began, Blackhawks **winger** Martin Havlat passed the puck to Toews. Toews worked around the side and tried to pass across the **crease** to Patrick Sharp. Instead the puck bounced off a Vancouver player and into the net. Score! Toews' goal marked the fifth and final lead change of the game. The Blackhawks were moving on in the Stanley Cup playoffs!

"I don't think anybody anticipated the craziness of the third period. The turns and swings were gigantic," said Chicago coach Joel Quenneville. "How it unraveled and unfolded, it was an amazing ending."

Toews finished the game with two goals and an assist. His game-winning goal was just a glimpse of what was to come for the budding young star.

winger—a type of forward who usually stays near the sides of the zone

crease—the area directly in front of the goal in hockey; it's often painted blue

With the win against Vancouver, Chicago moved on to the Western Conference finals for the first time in 14 years.

# CHAPTER 2

# A YOUNG LEADER

Jonathan Toews loved hockey even as a young boy. He was born April 29, 1988, in Winnipeg, Manitoba, Canada. He got his first pair of skates as a Christmas gift from his grandparents when he was 2 years old. Jonathan made his grandfather help him put his skates on first thing in the morning.

"My dad would say, 'We have to eat breakfast first and then we'll put your skates on,'" Jonathan's mother, Andree Gilbert, remembered. "Jonathan wasn't having any of that. He would say, 'No, we have to put the skates on first and then we'll eat breakfast.' So my dad would put (Jonathan's) skates on, and he would wear them in the house for the rest of the day, walking around pretending he was skating."

## A SPOKESMAN IS BORN

Jonathan's first skates came from a Canadian Tire store. Found throughout Canada, the stores sell everything from tools and car parts to clothes, shoes, and skates. Jonathan became a spokesman for Canadian Tire in 2010. As part of the

boys playing hockey on an outdoor rink in Winnipeg

agreement with Jonathan, the company started the Canadian Tire Hockey School (CTHS). The school is an online resource for kids and their parents. There also are six CTHS camps held throughout Canada where kids can learn hockey skills.

Jonathan's dad, Bryan Toews, took him skating in local hockey arenas. Bryan also built an ice rink in the back yard. He'd skate with Jonathan and his younger brother, David, and help them develop their hockey skills.

In 2003, while in high school, Jonathan was **drafted** Number 1 by the Tri-City Americans, a junior hockey team. Jonathan chose to stay home and play for his high school instead. His last two years of high school, Jonathan went to Shattuck-St. Mary's in Faribault, Minnesota. The school is known for developing outstanding hockey players. During his senior year, Jonathan racked up 110 **points** in 64 games and helped his team win the national midget championship.

He also was named captain of Canada's Team Western in 2005. At the world under-17 championships in Lethbridge, Alberta, Canada, Jonathan was the tournament's leading scorer with 12 points in six games. His team won the gold medal, and he was named tournament **MVP.**

draft—to choose a person to join a sports organization or team

points—a player's total number of goals and assists

MVP—stands for Most Valuable Player; an honor given to the best player in a tournament or during a season

## FAST FACT

Toews is not the only NHL star to come out of Shattuck-St. Mary's. Others who went to Shattuck include Sidney Crosby, Zach Parise, Derek Stepan

Jonathan proved he could be a leader in high school, and he did the same in college. After finishing high school in 2005, Jonathan spent two years at the University of North Dakota (UND). As a sophomore he was named an alternate captain. He led the UND Fighting Sioux to the Frozen Four in 2006 and 2007 and was chosen as an All-American. During his college career, Jonathan collected 85 points in 76 games.

During both college seasons, Jonathan also played for his home country at the International Ice Hockey Federation (IIHF) World Championships. Jonathan and Team Canada won gold each year. In 2007 he was Canada's leading scorer. He also notched a record three shoot-out goals in the semifinal game against the United States. That same year Jonathan made history. He became the first Canadian-born player to win gold medals at the World Junior Championship and the IIHF Senior World Championship in the same season.

But Jonathan was ready for even bigger things. The National Hockey League (NHL) waited.

shoot-out—a method of breaking a tie score at the end of overtime play

## A TALENTED LINE

Jonathan's linemates in college were Ryan Duncan and T.J. Oshie. Oshie went on to be a star for the St. Louis Blues. Duncan earned the Hobey Baker Award in 2007. The award is given each year to an outstanding college hockey player who shows leadership on and off the ice.

After he won the award, Duncan was asked how it felt to be the best college player in the country. He responded by saying he wasn't even the best player on his line.

Although he isn't fond on the nickname, Toews is often called Captain Serious.

# CHAPTER 3

# A RISING STAR IN THE NHL

The Chicago Blackhawks picked third in the 2006 NHL Draft. They took Toews.

Just 19 years old, Toews made his NHL **debut** in October 2007 against the San Jose Sharks. Toews made his presence known in the first period. Streaking toward the goal on a breakaway, he lofted the puck over the shoulder of San Jose's goalie. He scored on his first NHL shot! Toews went on to score a point in each of his first 10 games. For the season, he scored 24 goals and had 30 assists. But the Blackhawks struggled, though, and missed the playoffs.

Though he'd only finished his **rookie** season, Toews already had proved himself as a leader. Before the start of the next season, he was named team captain. At age 20 he was the youngest captain in Blackhawks history.

**debut**—a player's first game

**rookie**—a first-year player

Along with future stars Patrick Kane and Duncan Keith, Toews was part of an effort to bring more young talent to the Blackhawks. The effort quickly paid off. In the 2008–09 season, the trio helped Chicago qualify for the playoffs for the first time since 2002.

The Blackhawks defeated the Calgary Flames four games to two in the conference quarterfinals. They faced the Vancouver Canucks in the semifinals and won by the same margin. But a tough Detroit Red Wings team ended the Blackhawks' season four games to one. The season had been a great success, however, and even better things were in store for Blackhawks fans.

Toews collected 69 points in 82 games that year. He improved his face-off percentage to nearly 55 percent. He also earned his first trip to the All-Star Game in 2009.

The Blackhawks were on fire in 2009–10. They went 22 and 6 between November 9 and January 7, a tear that began with an eight-game winning streak. Toews netted 25 goals and 43 assists during the season.

## FAST FACT

*Toews scored a career-high 34 goals in 2008–09.*

Chicago finished 2009–10 in first place in the Central Division. They moved quickly through the playoffs. Chicago won four games to two against the Nashville Predators and Vancouver. In the conference semifinals, the Blackhawks downed the San Jose Sharks in four games.

Chicago faced the Philadelphia Flyers in the Stanley Cup Finals. After winning the first two games of the series, the Blackhawks dropped the next two. But Chicago wouldn't be denied. In Game 5 they won 7-4. The Flyers took the Blackhawks to overtime in Game 6, but Chicago pulled out the victory. Toews became the first Blackhawks captain in 49 years to hoist the Stanley Cup above his head in victory. And he earned it. During the playoffs he collected 29 points. He also won the Conn Smythe Trophy as the playoff MVP.

It was an amazing year for Toews. He also represented his country in the 2010 Olympics in Vancouver, British Columbia, Canada. Toews didn't disappoint. As the games got tougher, he only seemed to get better. Toews really showed his skills in a 7-3 win over Russia in the quarterfinals. His line helped shut down the Russians' most powerful line, which included NHL superstars Alexander Ovechkin and Evgeni Malkin.

After defeating Slovakia in the finals, Canada faced the United States in the gold medal game. In the preliminary rounds, the U.S. had handed Canada its only loss. Toews and Team Canada had no intention of letting that happen again.

Toews opened the scoring, shooting the puck past American goaltender Ryan Miller in the first period. Team Canada never trailed. They fought off a tough American team for an exciting 3-2 win, earning gold. Toews led his team with eight points and was named Best Forward of the tournament.

Toews got even better the next year. During the 2010–11 NHL season, he scored 32 goals and added 44 assists. His 76 points marked a career high. He also earned another trip to the All-Star Game.

Chicago played Vancouver in the playoff's first round. Tied at three games apiece, the series went to a deciding Game 7. Late in the game, Chicago trailed Vancouver 1-0. When the Blackhawks were called for a penalty, it looked as if the game was over. But with less than two minutes left in the game, Toews scored a shorthanded goal. The joy quickly turned to heartbreak when Vancouver scored in overtime. The Blackhawks' season was over.

**FAST FACT**

The 2010 gold medal game between Canada and the United States was the most-watched hockey game in the United States in 30 years. More than 27 million U.S. viewers tuned in.

The 2011–12 season was another rough one for the Blackhawks. They finished fourth in the Central Division. They were quickly knocked out of the playoffs by the Phoenix Coyotes. Toews' performance, however, earned him another trip to the All-Star Game.

The following season a dispute between players and owners resulted in a **lockout**. In the end, the NHL played a shortened schedule with just 48 regular season games. Once the season began, the Blackhawks tore through their opponents and finished first in the Central Division.

They proved just as unstoppable in the playoffs. They dropped the Minnesota Wild four games to one before facing the Detroit Red Wings. Though the Red Wings grabbed a three games to one lead, the Blackhawks wouldn't give up. Chicago won the next three games, the final one in overtime. Toews had one goal and three assists in the tight series.

After defeating the Los Angeles Kings four games to one, the Blackhawks moved on to the Stanley Cup Finals. They faced the Boston Bruins. The first game proved just how hard Toews and his team would have to work to repeat as champions. The Blackhawks won 4-3 in three overtimes. Game 2 went to overtime as well but was a 2-1 Bruins' win. After dropping Game 3, the Blackhawks bounced back for wins in games 4 and 6 to win the series. Toews scored a goal and added an assist to help his team to a 3-2 win in a dramatic Game 6 victory. Toews had carried his team to a second Stanley Cup championship!

lockout—a period of time in which owners prevent players from reporting to their teams; owners do not pay players during lockouts and no games are played

Toews has been nominated for the Frank J. Selke Trophy four times. He won it in 2013. The trophy is awarded to the NHL's best defensive forward.

**CHAPTER 4**

# GREAT EXPECTATIONS

Going into the 2013–14 season, the defending NHL champions looked like they'd be tough to beat. But they had their struggles during the season. From January 1 until the end of the regular season, the team had three losing streaks of three games or more. In the same timeframe, they had just one winning streak of more than two games.

But there were some bright spots. Toews stole the show when Chicago hosted an outdoor game against the Pittsburgh Penguins at Soldier Field March 1. Battling through wind and snow, he notched two goals and an assist in a 5-1 victory.

In March the injury bug struck the team, and Toews was not immune. He suffered an upper-body injury when he was **checked** into the boards in a game against the Penguins. He wouldn't be able to play for the rest of the regular season.

check—a legal hit with the body to try to force a player away from the puck

The Blackhawks finished the season in third place in the Central Division. They opened the playoffs against the St. Louis Blues. The Blackhawks looked like they were in trouble, dropping the first two games of the series.

But Toews helped his team storm back. Less than five minutes into Game 3, Toews crossed his blue line. With one defender in the way, Toews ripped a shot from the top of the left-hand circle. Goal! It was all Chicago would need to down the Blues. In Game 5, Toews scored on a breakaway to earn a 3-2 overtime win. He posted his third game-winning goal of the series in Game 7. The Blackhawks moved on to the conference semifinals.

Next Chicago faced the Minnesota Wild. With the series knotted at two games each, the teams were tied 1-1 in the third period of Game 5. Then Toews showcased his amazing strength and determination. After flattening forward Mikael Granlund, Toews went to the net. He fought off his defenders and knocked the puck past the Wild goalie. The goal was Toews' 10th playoff game-winner in his career.

The Blackhawks won Game 6 and moved on to meet the Los Angeles Kings. It proved to be a hard-fought seven-game series that included two overtime games. Game 7 went to the Kings in a 5-4 overtime win.

**FAST FACT**

*Toews has scored more game-winning goals during the playoffs than any other Blackhawks player in team history.*

Toews and Kane signed eight-year contracts worth about $84 million in July 2014. They said it was important to them to stay together along with their other Blackhawks teammates.

During his career Toews has shown he can do it all. He's a playmaker who scores goals and isn't afraid to deliver a big hit. He's dangerous in the face-off circle and is a strong penalty killer. Maybe most of all he's a leader. As captain of his team, Toews helped bring home two of the five Stanley Cup Championships in Blackhawks' history. And he's only getting started.

## FAST FACT

At the time, the contracts signed by Toews and Kane in 2014 paid them more per year than any other players in NHL history.

## SHOWING RESPECT

Sidney Crosby, captain of the Pittsburg Penguins, was asked to captain Canada's 2014 Olympic hockey team. He said he had to talk with Toews before he accepted. That's the level of respect other players have for him. Toews was named an alternate captain. Team Canada went on to win the gold medal.

# GLOSSARY

**center** (SEN-tur)—the player who participates in a face-off at the beginning of play

**check** (CHEK)—a legal hit with the body to try to force a player away from the puck

**crease** (KREES)—the area directly in front of the goal in hockey; it's often painted blue

**debut** (DAY-byoo)—a player's first game

**draft** (DRAFT)—to choose a person to join a sports organization or team

**lockout** (LOK-out)—a period of time in which owners prevent players from reporting to their teams; owners do not pay players during lockouts and no games are played

**MVP** (EM-VEE-PEE)—stands for Most Valuable Player; an honor given to the best player in a tournament or during a season

**penalty** (PEN-uhl-tee)—a punishment for breaking the rules

**points** (POYNTZ)—a player's total number of goals and assists

**power play** (POW-ur PLAY)—when a team has a one- or two-player advantage because the other team has one or more players in the penalty box

**rookie** (RUK-ee)—a first-year player

**shoot-out** (SHOOT-owt)—a method of breaking a tie score at the end of overtime play

**Stanley Cup** (STAN-lee KUP)—the trophy given each year to the NHL champion

**winger** (WING-ur)—a type of forward who usually stays near the sides of the zone

# READ MORE

**Christopher, Jordan.** *We Are the Goal Scorers: The Top Point Leaders of the NHL.* New York: Fenn/Tundra, 2013.

**Frederick, Shane.** *Six Degrees of Sidney Crosby: Connecting Hockey Stars.* Sports Illustrated Kids: Six Degrees of Sports. North Mankato, Minn.: Capstone Press, 2015.

**Gitlin, Marty.** *Hockey.* Best Sport Ever. Minneapolis: ABDO Pub., 2012.

# INTERNET SITES

FactHound offers a safe, fun way to find Internet sites related to this book. All of the sites on FactHound have been researched by our staff.

Here's all you do:

Visit *www.facthound.com*

Type in this code: 9781620651575

**Super-cool stuff!** Check out projects, games and lots more at **www.capstonekids.com**

# INDEX